MW01105336

**To:**

_____

**From:**

_____

**Date:**

_____

*For a #1 Dad*

© 2013  Christian Art Gifts, RSA
         Christian Art Gifts Inc., IL, USA

Designed by Christian Art Gifts

Images used under license from Shutterstock.com

Printed in China

ISBN 978-1-4321-0460-3

13   14   15   16   17   18   19   20   21   22   –   10   9   8   7   6   5   4   3   2   1

For a #1 DAD

christian art gifts ®

The greatest thing a man
can do for his heavenly Father
is to be kind to some of
His other children.
{ Henry Drummond }

Pursue
RIGHTEOUS LIVING,
FAITHFULNESS,
LOVE, and PEACE.
Enjoy the companionship
of those who call on the
Lord with pure hearts.
{ 2 Tim. 2:22 }

Pay careful attention to your own work, for then you will get the satisfaction of a job well done, and you won't need to compare yourself to anyone else.

{ Gal. 6:4 }

A child is not likely to find a
**FATHER IN GOD** unless he finds
something of **GOD IN HIS FATHER.**
{ Austin L. Sorenson }

There is no fear in love.
But perfect love drives out fear.

{ 1 John 4:18 }

8

A person's attitude toward himself has a profound
influence on his attitude toward God, his family, his friends,
his future, and many other significant areas of his life.
{ Bill Gothard }

Christ alone can bring us
**lasting peace** –
peace with God –
peace among men and nations –
and peace within our hearts.

{ Billy Graham }

**SUCCESS** is not final,
failure is not fatal:
it is the **COURAGE** to
continue that counts.

{ Winston Churchill }

The Lord will give
**strength** to His people;
the Lord will
**bless** His people with
**peace**.

{ Ps. 29:11 }

**Whatever you are,**

**be a good one.**

{ Abraham Lincoln }

We know that in
all things God works
for the good of
those who love Him,
who have been
called according
to His purpose.

{ Rom. 8:28 }

He didn't
tell me
how to live;

he lived and
let me watch
him do it.
{ Clarence Kelland }

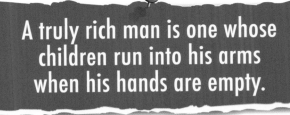

A truly rich man is one whose children run into his arms when his hands are empty.

The Lᴏʀᴅ
will give
**STRENGTH**
to His people;
the Lᴏʀᴅ will
**BLESS** His
people with
**PEACE.**
{ Ps. 29:11 }

Any man can be a father. It takes **SOMEONE SPECIAL** to be a dad.

There are no adequate
substitutes for father, mother,
and children bound together
in a loving commitment
to nurture and protect.
No government, no matter
how well-intentioned, can take
the place of the family in
the scheme of things.

{ Gerald Ford }

**COURAGE** is what it takes
to stand up and speak;
**COURAGE** is also what it takes
to sit down and listen.
{ Winston Churchill }

# To be yourself in a world that is constantly trying to make you something else is the greatest accomplishment.

{ Ralph Waldo Emerson }

The quality of a
person's life is in
direct proportion
to their commitment
to excellence,
regardless of their
chosen field
of endeavor.

{ Vincent T. Lombardi }

The **earnest prayer** of a righteous person has great power and produces wonderful results.

{ James 5:16 }

Dad, your guiding hand on my shoulder will remain with me forever. As for me and my house, WE WILL SERVE THE LORD. { Josh. 24:15 }

My help comes from the LORD,

who made heaven and earth. { Ps. 121:2 }

Jesus Christ
is the same
yesterday,
today,
and
forever.

{ Heb. 13:8 }

IT IS NEVER TOO
LATE TO BE WHAT YOU
MIGHT HAVE BEEN.
{ George Eliot }

You are **never** too old
to set another **goal**
or to dream a
new **dream.**

{ C. S. Lewis }

Endurance produces
**CHARACTER,**
and
character produces
**HOPE.**

{ Rom. 5:4 }

**No power in the sky above or in the earth below – indeed, nothing in all creation will ever be able to separate us from the love of God that is revealed in Christ Jesus our Lord.**

{ Rom. 8:39 }

**TEACH ME TO DO YOUR WILL,** for You are my God! Let Your good Spirit lead me on level ground!

{ Ps. 143:10 }